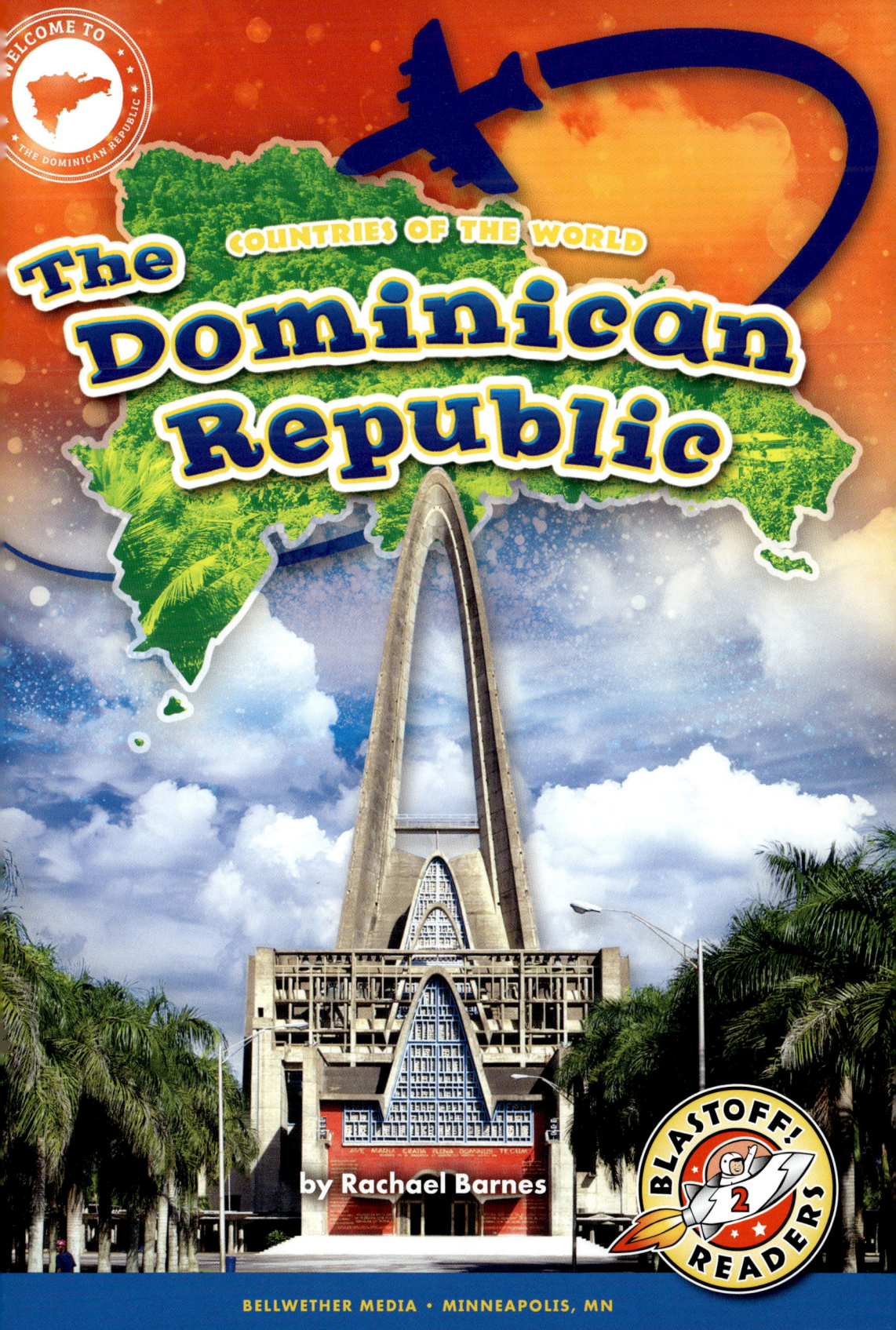

Blastoff! Readers are carefully developed by literacy experts to build reading stamina and move students toward fluency by combining standards-based content with developmentally appropriate text.

LEVELS

Level 1 provides the most support through repetition of high-frequency words, light text, predictable sentence patterns, and strong visual support.

Level 2 offers early readers a bit more challenge through varied sentences, increased text load, and text-supportive special features.

Level 3 advances early-fluent readers toward fluency through increased text load, less reliance on photos, advancing concepts, longer sentences, and more complex special features.

★ **Blastoff! Universe**

Reading Level

Grade K

Grades 1–3

Grade 4

This edition first published in 2023 by Bellwether Media, Inc.

No part of this publication may be reproduced in whole or in part without written permission of the publisher. For information regarding permission, write to Bellwether Media, Inc., Attention: Permissions Department, 6012 Blue Circle Drive, Minnetonka, MN 55343.

Library of Congress Cataloging-in-Publication Data

Names: Barnes, Rachael, author.
Title: The Dominican Republic / by Rachael Barnes.
Description: Minneapolis, MN : Bellwether Media, 2023. | Series: Blastoff! Readers: Countries of the world | Includes bibliographical references and index. | Audience: Ages 5-8 | Audience: Grades 2-3 | Summary: "Relevant images match informative text in this introduction to the Dominican Republic. Intended for students in kindergarten through third grade"-- Provided by publisher.
Identifiers: LCCN 2022044254 (print) | LCCN 2022044255 (ebook) | ISBN 9798886871289 (library binding) | ISBN 9798886872545 (ebook)
Subjects: LCSH: Dominican Republic--Juvenile literature.
Classification: LCC F1934.2 .B376 2023 (print) | LCC F1934.2 (ebook) | DDC 972.93--dc23/eng/20220913
LC record available at https://lccn.loc.gov/2022044254
LC ebook record available at https://lccn.loc.gov/2022044255

Text copyright © 2023 by Bellwether Media, Inc. BLASTOFF! READERS and associated logos are trademarks and/or registered trademarks of Bellwether Media, Inc.

Editor: Elizabeth Neuenfeldt   Designer: Gabriel Hilger

Printed in the United States of America, North Mankato, MN.

Table of Contents

All About the Dominican Republic	4
Land and Animals	6
Life in the Dominican Republic	12
Dominican Republic Facts	20
Glossary	22
To Learn More	23
Index	24

All About the Dominican Republic

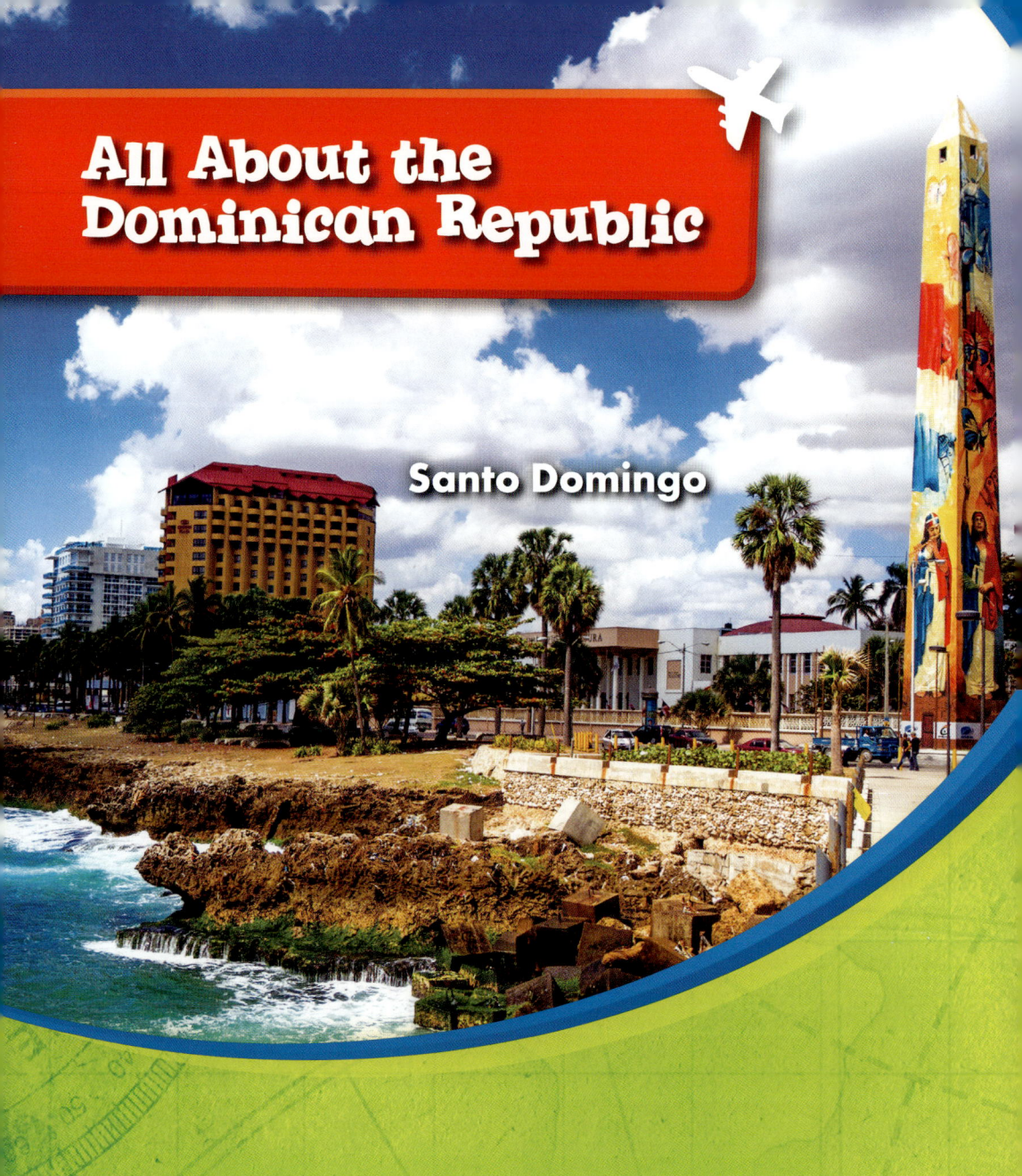

Santo Domingo

The Dominican Republic is on a large island. It is in the Caribbean Sea.

Santo Domingo is the capital. It is one of the oldest cities in the Caribbean!

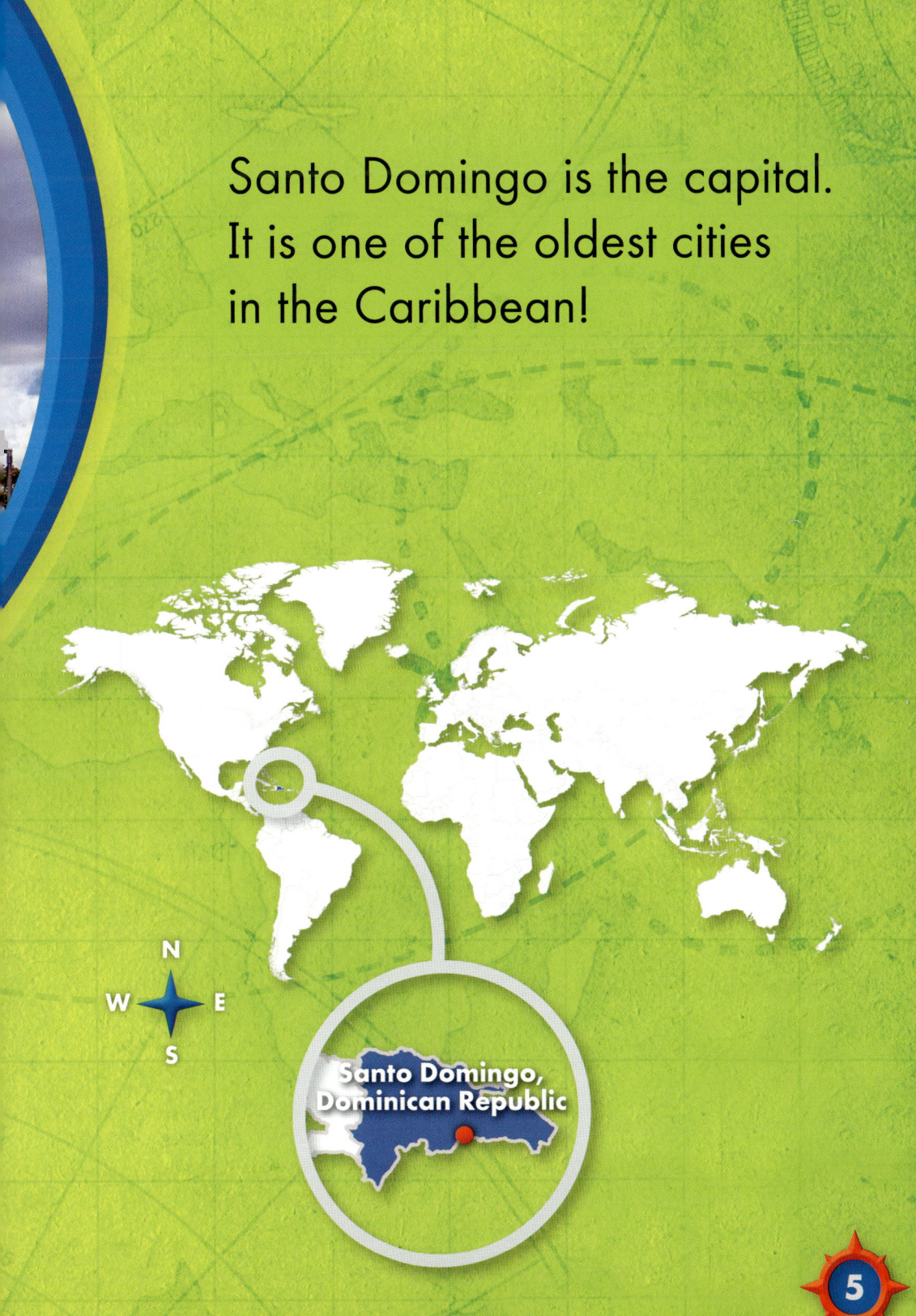

Land and Animals

Mountains cover the Dominican Republic. Duarte Peak is the tallest. Valleys and **plains** spread out around the mountains.

Lake Enriquillo sits in the southwest. Palm trees grow on coastal beaches.

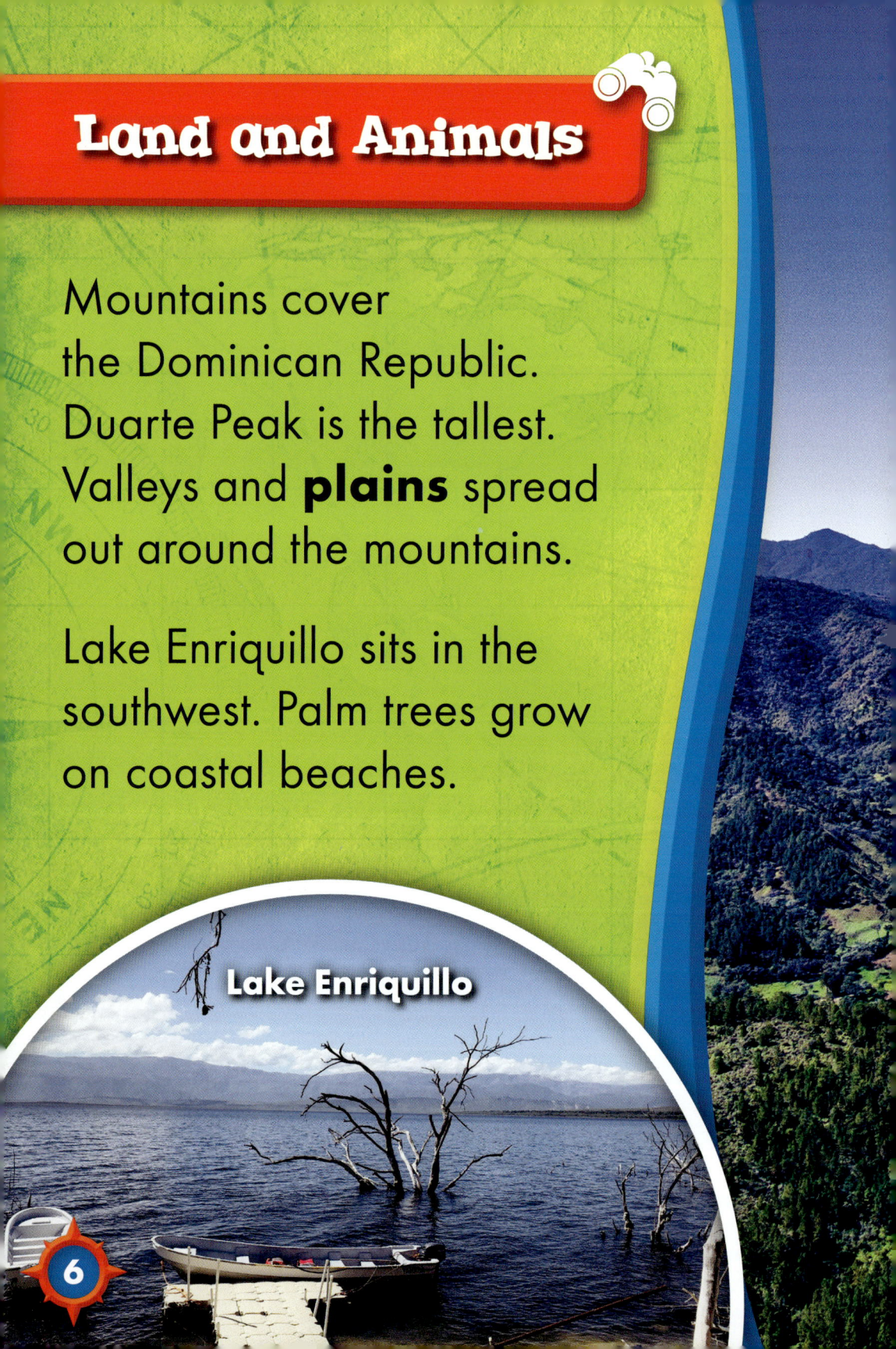

Lake Enriquillo

Duarte Peak

Size: 10,417 feet (3,175 meters) tall

Famous For:
tallest mountain in the Caribbean

Most of the country is warm and **humid**. More rain falls in summer. Less rain falls in winter.

Hurricanes sometimes blow in from the Atlantic Ocean.

Hummingbirds fly in mountain forests. Palmchats nest in palm trees. Lizards race along beaches.

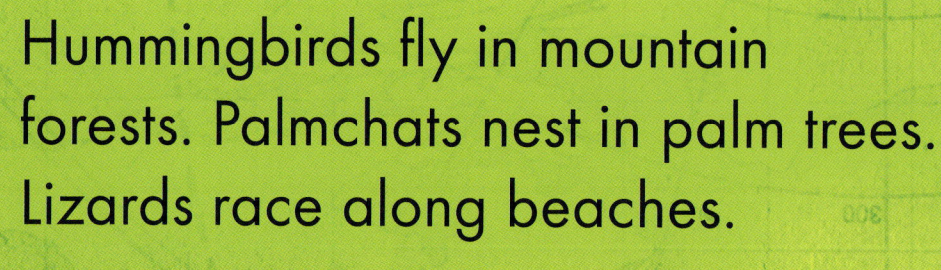

Santo Domingo curlytail lizard

Animals of the Dominican Republic

hummingbird

palmchat

American crocodile

West Indian manatee

Crocodiles hunt in Lake Enriquillo's salty water. Manatees eat ocean plants.

Life in the Dominican Republic

Most Dominicans have mixed **heritage**. They have European and African backgrounds. Many people live in big cities.

Dominicans mostly speak Spanish. Many are **Catholics**.

Catholic church

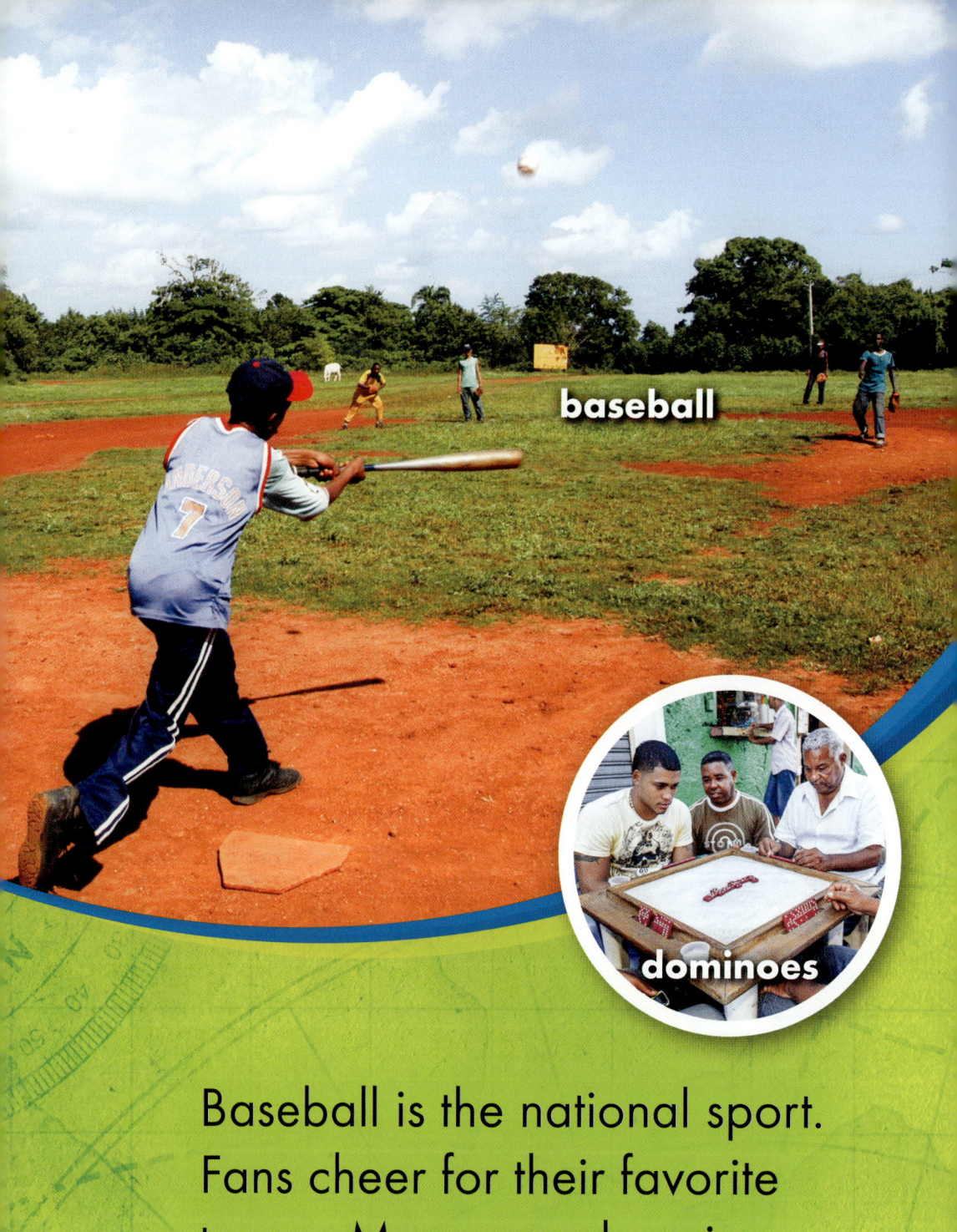

Baseball is the national sport. Fans cheer for their favorite teams. Many people enjoy playing dominoes.

Merengue is a kind of music and dance. People play it at **festivals**!

merengue musicians

La Bandera is a favorite Dominican dish. It has rice, beans, and meat. *Sancocho* is a tasty stew.

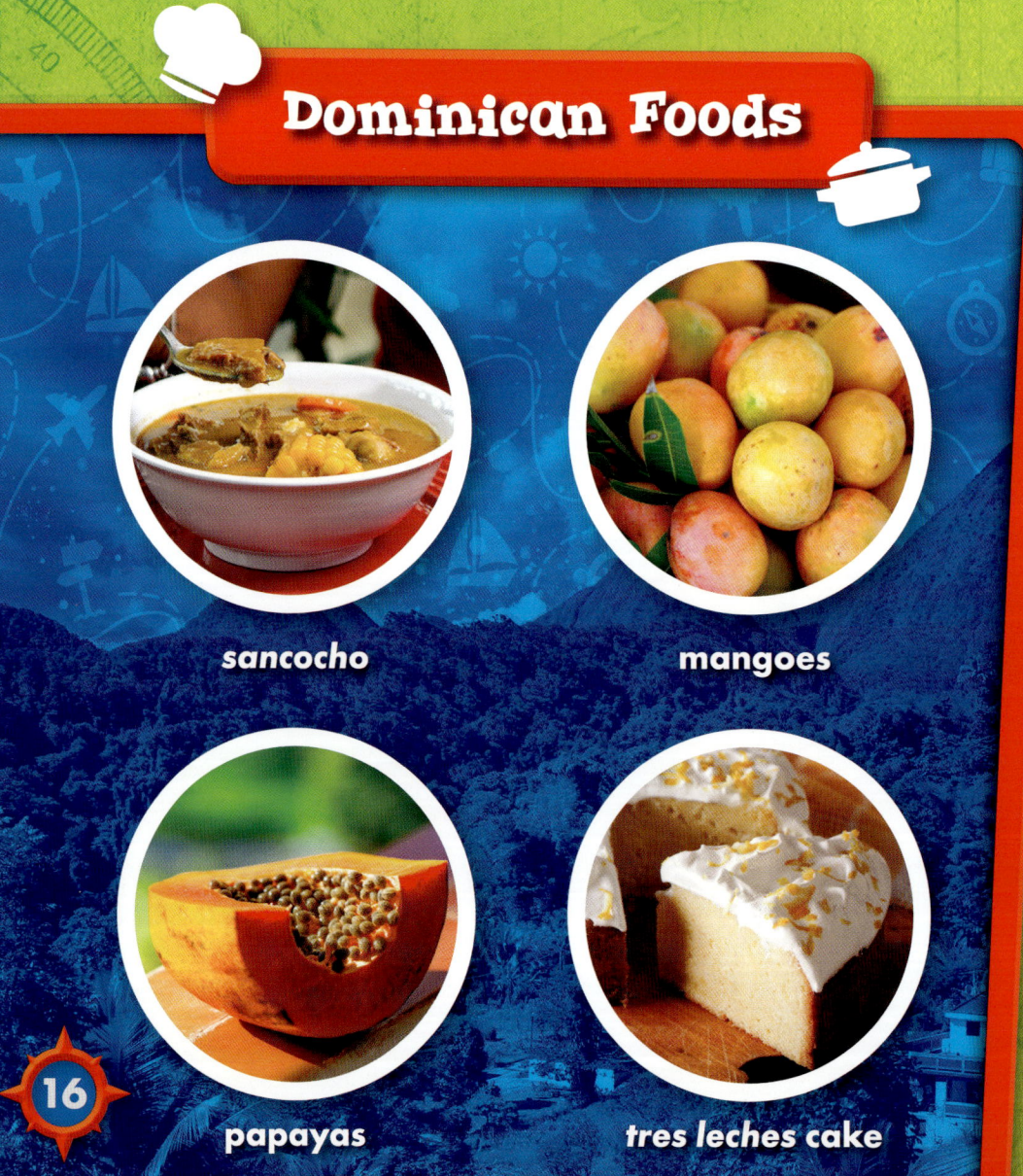

Dominican Foods

sancocho

mangoes

papayas

tres leches cake

People enjoy mangoes and papayas. *Tres leches* cake is a sweet treat!

El Carnaval

People **celebrate** *El Carnaval* in winter. Dominicans dress up and dance at parades!

On New Year's Eve, families eat together. The Dominican Republic has many joyful holidays!

Dominican Republic Facts

Size:
18,792 square miles
(48,670 square kilometers)

Population:
10,694,700 (2022)

National Holiday:
Independence Day (February 27)

Main Language:
Spanish

Capital City:
Santo Domingo

Famous Face

Name: Juan Luis Guerra
Famous For: award-winning musician known for his merengue music

Religions

Roman Catholic: 44%

none: 29%

other Christian: 22%

other: 5%

Top Landmarks

Columbus Lighthouse

Lake Enriquillo

Salto El Limón

Glossary

Catholics—people belonging or relating to the Christian church that is led by the pope

celebrate—to do something special or fun for an event, occasion, or holiday

festivals—times or events of celebration

heritage—the backgrounds and beliefs that are part of the history of a group of people

humid—having a lot of water in the air

hurricanes—tropical storms with high winds, rain, thunder, and lightning

plains—large areas of flat land

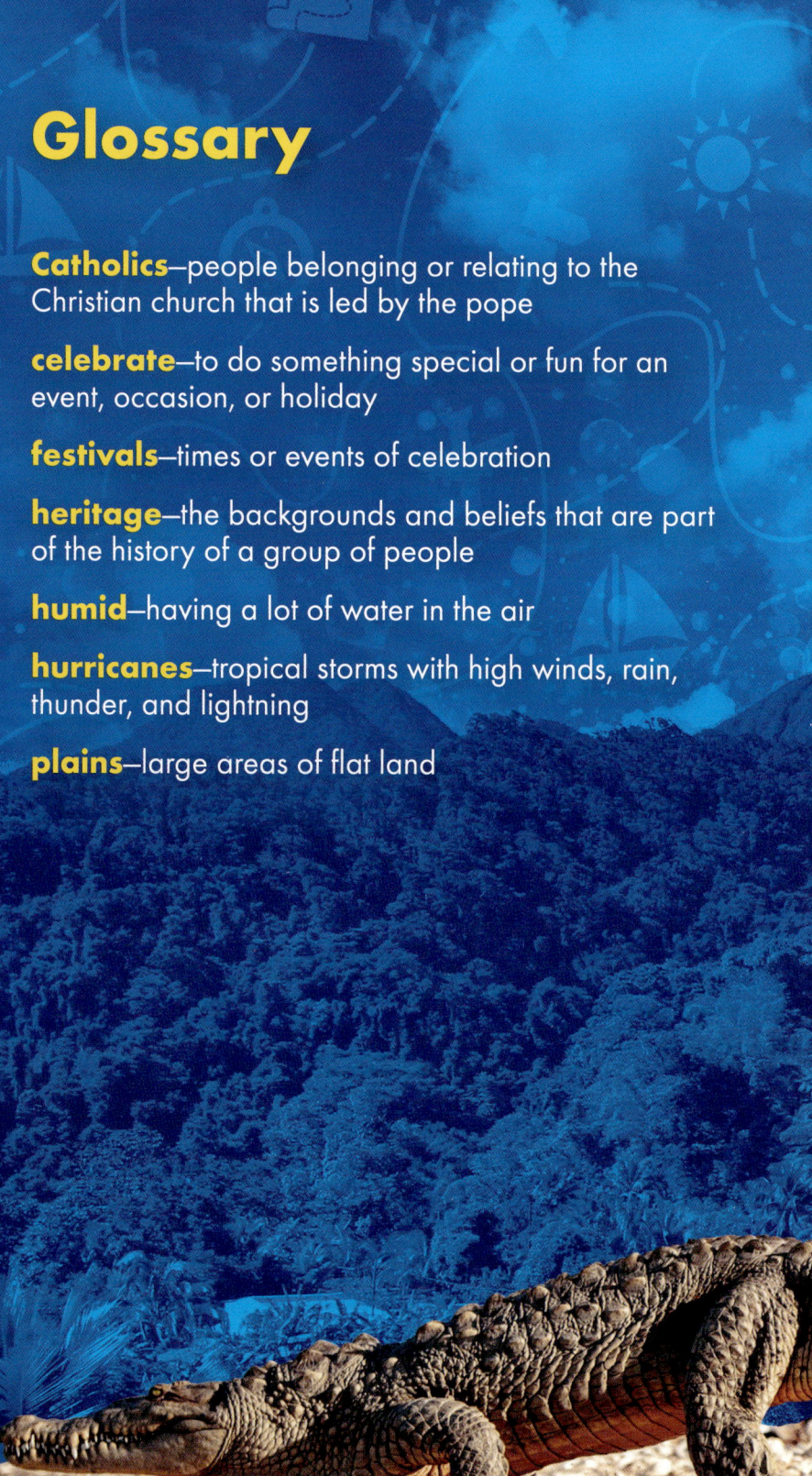

To Learn More

AT THE LIBRARY

Cipriano, Jeri. *Dominican Republic*. Egremont, Mass.: Red Chair Press, 2019.

Dean, Jessica. *Dominican Republic*. Minneapolis, Minn.: Jump!, 2019.

Rathburn, Betsy. *Hurricanes*. Minneapolis, Minn.: Bellwether Media, 2020.

ON THE WEB

FACTSURFER

Factsurfer.com gives you a safe, fun way to find more information.

1. Go to www.factsurfer.com.
2. Enter "the Dominican Republic" into the search box and click 🔍.
3. Select your book cover to see a list of related content.

Index

animals, 10, 11
Atlantic Ocean, 9
baseball, 14
beaches, 6, 10
capital (see Santo Domingo)
Caribbean Sea, 4, 5
Catholics, 12
cities, 5, 12
Dominican Republic facts, 20–21
dominoes, 14
Duarte Peak, 6, 7
El Carnaval, 18
foods, 16, 17
hurricanes, 9
island, 4
Lake Enriquillo, 6, 11
map, 5
merengue, 15
mountains, 6, 10
New Year's Eve, 19
people, 12, 14, 15, 17, 18
plains, 6
rain, 8
Santo Domingo, 4, 5
say hello, 13
Spanish, 12, 13
summer, 8
valleys, 6
winter, 8, 18

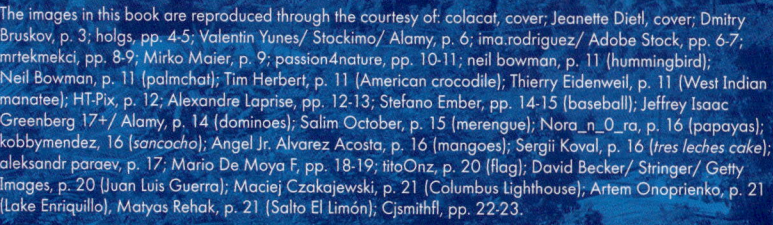

The images in this book are reproduced through the courtesy of: colacat, cover; Jeanette Dietl, cover; Dmitry Bruskov, p. 3; holgs, pp. 4-5; Valentin Yunes/ Stockimo/ Alamy, p. 6; ima.rodriguez/ Adobe Stock, pp. 6-7; mrtekmekci, pp. 8-9; Mirko Maier, p. 9; passion4nature, pp. 10-11; neil bowman, p. 11 (hummingbird); Neil Bowman, p. 11 (palmchat); Tim Herbert, p. 11 (American crocodile); Thierry Eidenweil, p. 11 (West Indian manatee); HT-Pix, p. 12; Alexandre Laprise, pp. 12-13; Stefano Ember, pp. 14-15 (baseball); Jeffrey Isaac Greenberg 17+/ Alamy, p. 14 (dominoes); Salim October, p. 15 (merengue); Nora_n_0_ra, p. 16 (papayas); kobbymendez, 16 (*sancocho*); Angel Jr. Alvarez Acosta, p. 16 (mangoes); Sergii Koval, p. 16 (*tres leches cake*); aleksandr paraev, p. 17; Mario De Moya F, pp. 18-19; titoOnz, p. 20 (flag); David Becker/ Stringer/ Getty Images, p. 20 (Juan Luis Guerra); Maciej Czakajewski, p. 21 (Columbus Lighthouse); Artem Onoprienko, p. 21 (Lake Enriquillo), Matyas Rehak, p. 21 (Salto El Limón); Cjsmithfl, pp. 22-23.

24